This book is a collection of affirmations and heartfelt messages, a token of appreciation for the countless ways mothers shape our lives with love, wisdom, and strength.

Remember the Love

I am grateful for the unconditional
love you have always shown me.

Remember the Love

I am thankful for the sacrifices
you have made to provide for me.

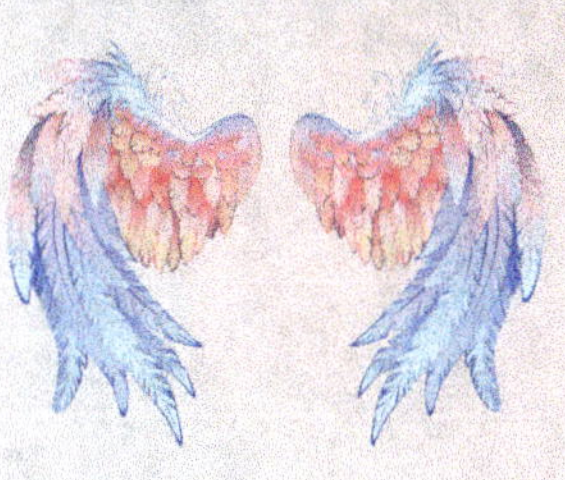

Remember the Love

I love and appreciate you for your
nurturing and caring nature.

Remember the Love

I am blessed to have a mother who supports me in pursuing my dreams.

Remember the Love

I am grateful for the wisdom and guidance you impart on me.

Remember the Love

I cherish the special moments spent with you, filled with love and laughter.

Remember the Love

I am thankful for the strength and resilience you demonstrate in facing challenges.

Remember the Love

Remember the Love

I love you for always believing in
me and encouraging me to be my
best self.

Remember the Love

I am grateful for the warm hugs
and comforting presence of you.

Remember the Love

Remember the Love

I appreciate your kindness and compassion towards others.

Remember the Love

I am thankful for the lessons of love and compassion you teach me every day.

Remember the Love

Remember the Love

I love you for the unwavering support and encouragement you provide.

Remember the Love

Remember the Love

I am grateful for the endless love
and devotion you shower upon me.

Remember the Love

I cherish the memories of laughter
and joy shared with you.

Remember the Love

Remember the Love

I am thankful for the strength and
resilience that you instill in me.

Remember the Love

Remember the Love

I love you for your selflessness and
generosity towards others.

Remember the Love

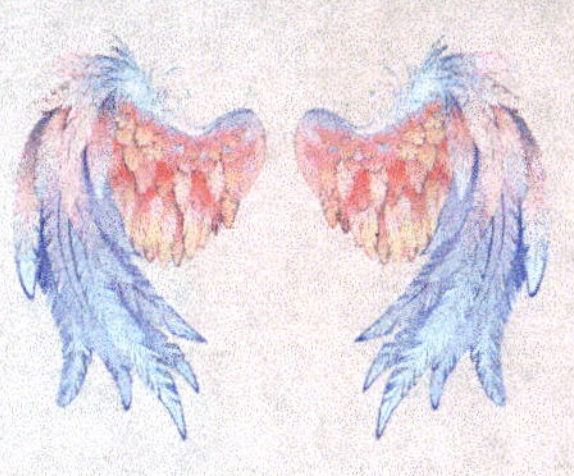

Remember the Love

I am grateful for the bond of love
and understanding I share with
you.

Remember the Love

Remember the Love

I appreciate you for the sacrifices
you make to ensure my happiness.

Remember the Love

Remember the Love

I am thankful for the
unconditional love and acceptance I
receive from you.

Remember the Love

I love you for your unwavering
faith in me and my abilities.

Remember the Love

Remember the Love

I am grateful for the guidance and
wisdom you provide me with.

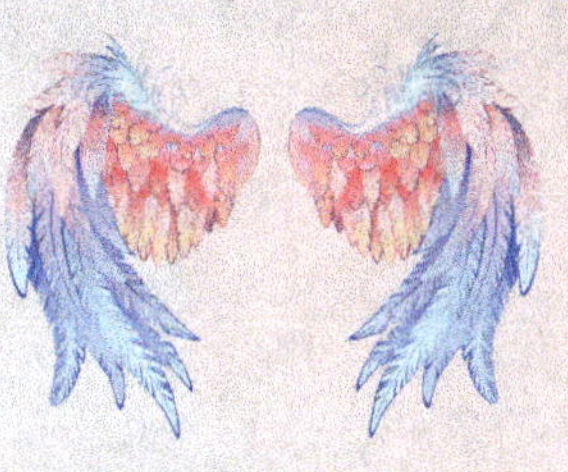

Remember the Love

I appreciate you for your patience
and understanding during difficult
times.

Remember the Love

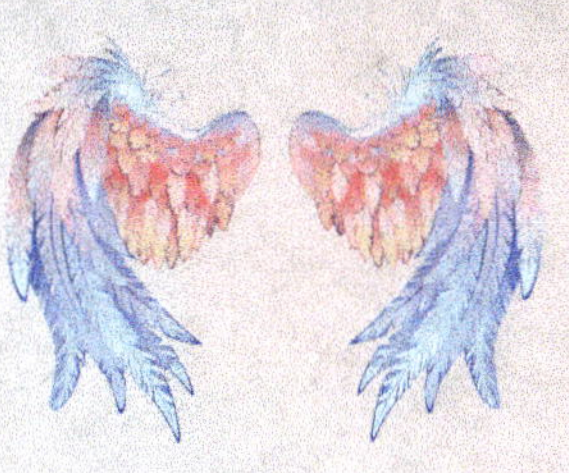

Remember the Love

I am thankful for the laughter and
joy you bring into my life.

Remember the Love

I love you for your endless devotion
and dedication to our family.

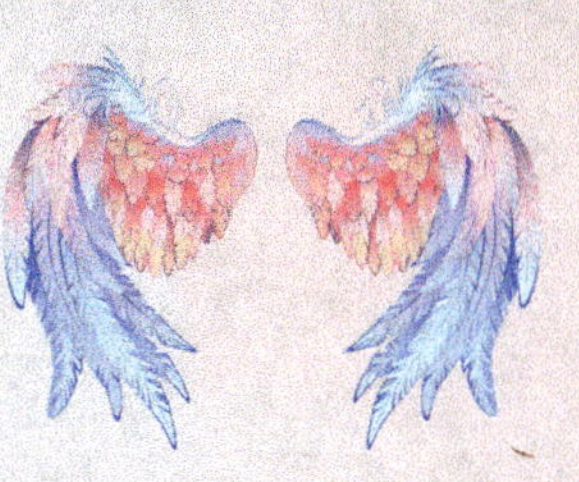

Remember the Love

I am grateful for the lessons of resilience and perseverance you teach me.

Remember the Love

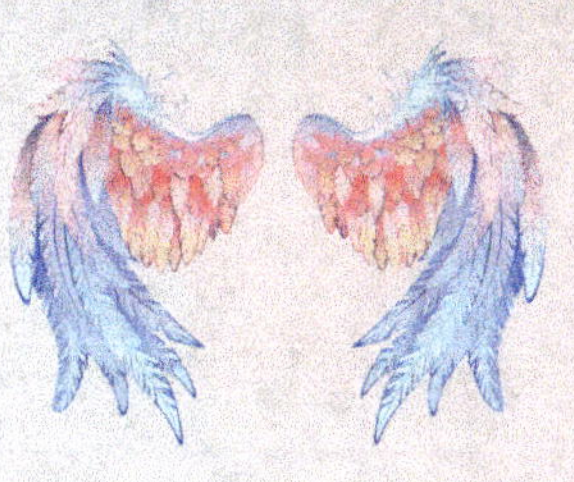

Remember the Love

I appreciate you for the love and
care you show towards everyone
around you.

Remember the Love

Remember the Love

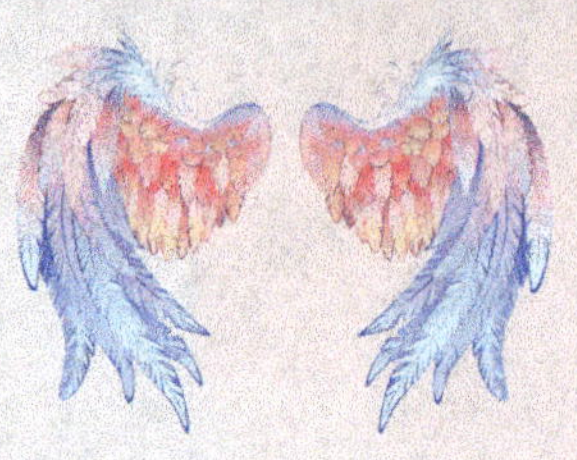

I am thankful for the strength and courage you demonstrate in facing challenges.

Remember the Love

I love you for your kindness and
compassion towards others.

Remember the Love

I am grateful for the bond of love
and trust I share with you.

Remember the Love

Remember the Love

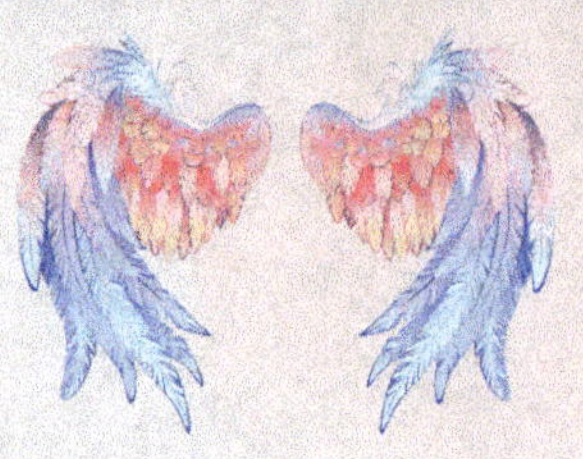

I appreciate you for the support and encouragement you give me in pursuing my dreams.

Remember the Love

I am thankful for the wisdom and
guidance you impart on me.

Remember the Love

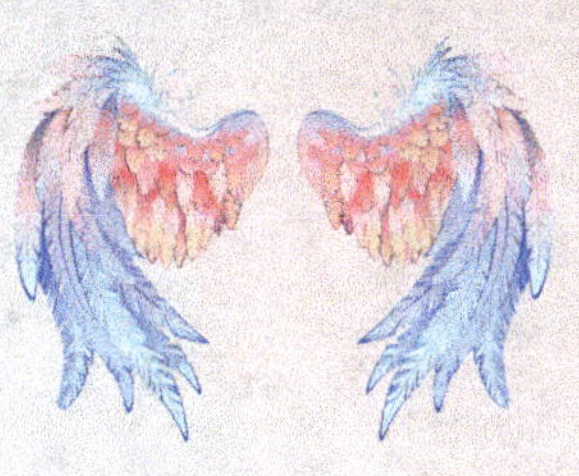

Remember the Love

I love you for your unwavering
belief in my potential.

Remember the Love

I am thankful for the love and
care you show me every day.

Remember the Love

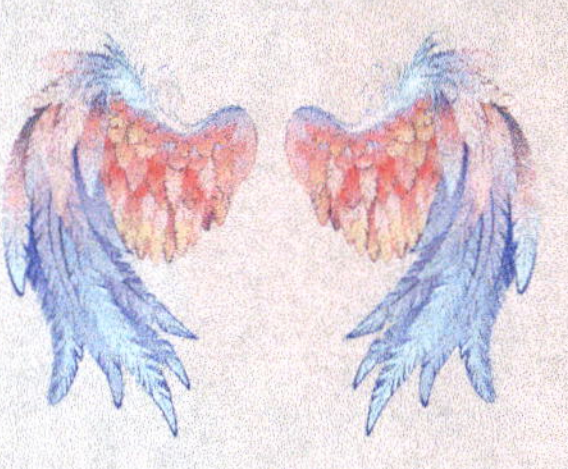

Remember the Love

I love you for your strength and
resilience in facing challenges.

Remember the Love

Remember the Love

I am grateful for the lessons of
kindness and compassion you teach
me.

Remember the Love

I appreciate you for the sacrifices
you make to ensure my well-being.

Remember the Love

Remember the Love

I appreciate you for the support
and encouragement you give to me.

Remember the Love

Remember the Love

I am thankful for the wisdom and
guidance you offer me.

Remember the Love

Remember the Love

I love you for your unwavering
belief in my abilities.

Remember the Love

Remember the Love

I am grateful for the laughter and
joy you bring into my life.

Remember the Love

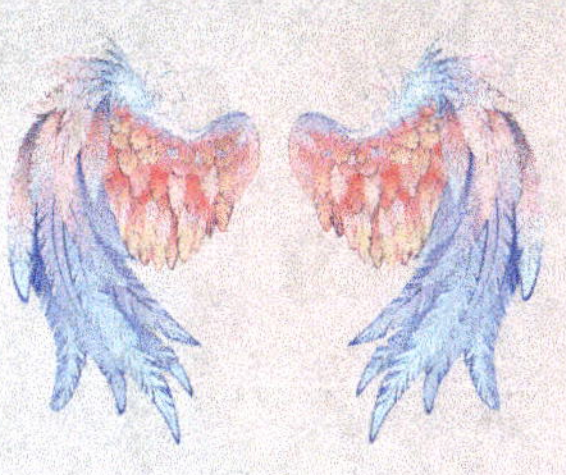

Remember the Love

I appreciate you for the support
and encouragement you provide me
with.

Remember the Love

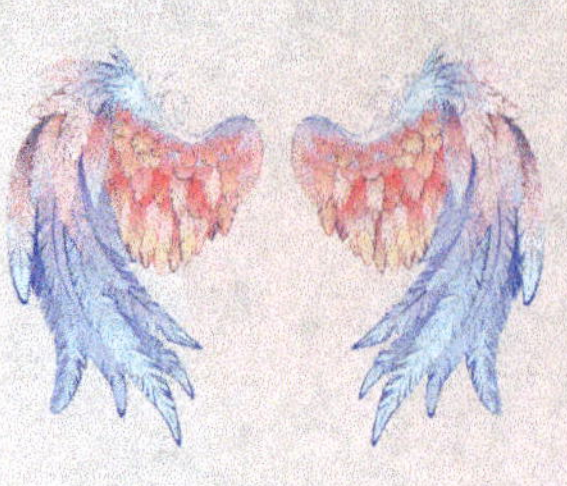

Remember the Love

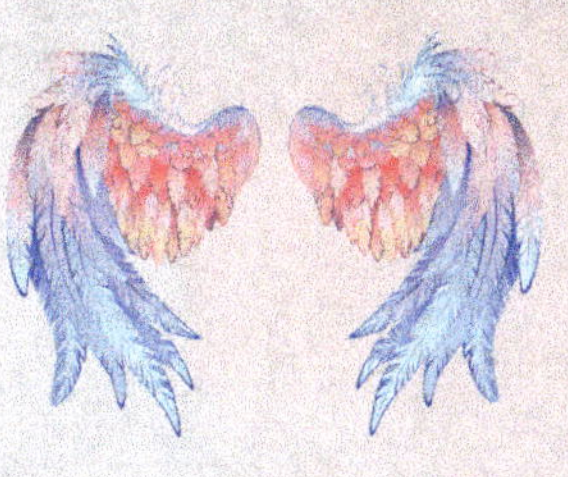

Remember the Love

Dedicated to My Mother

I Remember the Love